Come to the Table

A Resource Book for Holy Communion

MARTY PARKS

Lillenas PUBLISHING COMPANY

KANSAS CITY, MO 64141

Published by Lillenas Publishing Company, Kansas City, MO 64141
Printed in the United States of America

Cover Design by Ted Ferguson

10   9   8   7   6   5   4   3   2   1

Contents

Introduction   5

1. Opening Sentences   7

2. Unison/Responsive Scriptures, Readings, and Prayers   9

3. Foundational Scriptures for Communion   20

4. Appropriate Hymns for Communion   24

5. Appropriate Worship Songs for Communion   27

6. Appropriate Choral Anthems for Communion   29

7. Creative Ideas for Communion   31

8. Service Orders of Worship   33

Sources and References   38

Introduction

Have we lost the significance of Holy Communion? Has the Lord's Supper become only a memorial service with no reference given to the triumphant victory of Christ's redemptive act? Has the Eucharist been transformed into a lifeless ritual with no spirit of thanksgiving in evidence?

Though it goes by different names according to our different traditions and customs, sharing in the bread and cup reminds us of the sacrificial death of Jesus, imparting grace-filled life to the believer. On that we can all agree!

This high and holy observance (or ordinance, or sacrament) is, most assuredly, a means of grace; an ordinary channel through which we experience the extraordinary grace of God. At the Table of the Lord, Jesus Christ is spiritually present and the gospel is enacted. We reflect on His death and we rejoice in His salvation. We mourn His suffering yet we exult in His final victory. We commemorate His act of deliverance and we celebrate our ultimate destiny. In short, we remember the future.

We call it *The Lord's Supper* based on Christ's last meal shared with His disciples the night He was betrayed. He instructed them to eat and drink the bread and the wine, which He said were His own body and blood, broken and poured out for many. Just as that meal, in the Passover tradition, was a reenactment of God's deliverance of the Israelites from Egyptian slavery, our participation in the Lord's Supper allows us to reenact God's salvation from sin and death through His Son, Jesus Christ (see Mark 14:22-24).

We call it *Holy Communion* because we share *with* the community of believers and in the sacrifice of Christ. It is indeed holy, set apart for God. Further, it is because of His Son that we share life in Him and with each other. Christ has brought us together—we are one in Him (see 1 Corinthians 10:16—17).

We call it *The Eucharist,* a word meaning "thanksgiving" and having its roots in the second chapter of Acts. There we read that the fellowship of believers met daily in the temple courts and ate together in their homes with thankful and sincere hearts. In the

5

midst of all we have to be thankful for, nothing compares to expressions of thanks for the person and work of Jesus Christ who himself gave thanks at the Last Supper. Introspection should always be balanced with thanksgiving (see Acts 2:46).

So, no matter what you call it, the Lord's Supper or Holy Communion or the Eucharist, please respond to *the call* . . . and come to the table.

Come to the Table is intended to be a resource of ideas and applications for pastors, worship leaders, and others who design and implement worship, especially worship around the Lord's Table. Because we all do things differently, not every idea presented here will be useful for every congregation. In fact, the elements in this book have been drawn from a broad spectrum of denominations, traditions, and sources—some ancient, some contemporary. Most likely no one will be able to use them all. Yet probably everyone will find several things that will serve as starting points to spark creativity and bring enhancement to this vital moment in Christian worship.

I am deeply indebted to Rev. Jim Genesse and Rev. Steve Blakemore for their generous sharing of insight, wisdom, and experience. I am also grateful to Pat Jones for her organizational skills in the compiling of this book's contents.

—Marty Parks

Opening Sentences for Communion

The moment has come. A celebration is about to occur. The Master has prepared it. Only He could set this table; only He could send out the invitation; and He has done both. Come then, you who declare Jesus as your King. Come share in this celebration of the breaking of the bread and the drinking of the wine, and remember the sacrifice of Jesus, which was the cost of setting this table.

(CUMC)

Let all who have repented of their sins, who have accepted Jesus Christ as their personal Savior and Lord, and who are in fellowship with his church, receive with thanksgiving the bread and cup, in remembrance of our crucified and resurrected Lord.   (BWH, 119)

Brothers and sisters in Christ, the Gospels tell us that on the first day of the week, the day on which our Lord rose from the dead, He appeared to some of his disciples and was made known to them in the breaking of bread. Come, then, to the joyful feast of our Lord.

(CRPH)

The Lord's Supper is a rich reminder and confirming seal of new life in Christ. Receiving the bread and drinking the cup in faith brings us assurance that His body was broken for us and His blood poured out on our behalf. What is more, He is forever our nourishment and strength. A remembrance, yes; but also a celebration!

(CUMC)

Jesus prayed for His disciples and for us when He asked that the Father make us one in Him. Even then, centuries ago, you were a concern to Him. Today in the breaking of the bread and drinking of the cup, may you experience again the presence of the living Christ who has loved us, through His death, to life everlasting.   (CUMC)

The sacrament of Holy Communion has been described as a "remembering of the future." May God open the eyes of your heart today, that you may see anew the One who, through His sacrifice and precious blood, has prepared a place for us to dwell with Him . . . forever.   (CUMC)

LEADER: The grace of the Lord Jesus Christ be with you.

CONGREGATION: **And also with you.**

LEADER: The Risen Christ is with us.

CONGREGATION: **Praise the Lord.**

LEADER: And so, we offer ourselves in praise and thanksgiving as a holy and living sacrifice, in union with Christ's offering for us, as we proclaim the mystery of faith:

CONGREGATION: **Christ has died; Christ is risen; Christ will come again!**

LEADER: The Lord is with His people;
       Now may He be with you.

CONGREGATION: **The Lord is with His servants;
       May He be with you too.**

LEADER: Now lift your hearts to praise Him.

CONGREGATION: **To God we lift them high.
       'Tis right to praise and thank Him
       Who to His world draws nigh.**

       (CC)

Unison and Responsive Scriptures, Readings, and Prayers for Communion

Almighty God, unto whom all hearts are open, all desires known, and from whom no secrets are hid; Cleanse the thoughts of our hearts by the inspiration of thy Holy Spirit, that we may perfectly love thee, and worthily magnify thy holy Name; through Christ our Lord. Amen.   BCP, 67

Ye who do truly and earnestly repent you of your sins, and are in love and charity with your neighbors, and intend to lead a new life, following the commandments of God, and walking from henceforth in his holy ways; Draw near with faith, and take this holy Sacrament to your comfort; and make your humble confession to Almighty God.   BCP, 75

Almighty God, creator, ruler and judge of all: We confess that we all have sinned and fallen short of Your glory. In earnest repentance we come to You, for even the remembrance of our sin is grievous to us. Still, we acknowledge that in You is mercy and forgiveness. We ask that, through Your grace, we Your people may from this moment serve and please You to the honor and glory of Your name; through Jesus Christ, Your Son and our Lord. Amen.

The Great Thanksgiving

The Lord be with you.
And also with you.
Lift up your hearts.
We lift them up to the Lord.
Let us give thanks to the Lord our God.
It is right to give our thanks and praise.
It is right, and a good and joyful thing,
always and everywhere to give thanks to you,
Father Almighty, creator of heaven and earth.

And so,
    with your people on earth
    and all the company of heaven
    we praise your name and join their unending hymn:

Holy, holy, holy Lord, God of power and might,
heaven and earth are full of your glory,
    Hosanna in the highest.
Blessed is he who comes in the name of the LORD.
    Hosanna in the highest.

Prayer of Confession and Pardon

Merciful God,
we confess that we have not loved you with our whole heart.
We have failed to be an obedient church.
We have not done your will,
we have broken your law,
we have rebelled against your love,
we have not loved our neighbors,
and we have not heard the cry of the needy.
Forgive us, we pray.
Free us for joyful obedience,
through Jesus Christ our Lord. Amen.

The Apostles' Creed

I believe in God the Father Almighty, maker of heaven and earth;
And in Jesus Christ his only Son our Lord:
Who was conceived by the Holy Spirit,
Born of the Virgin Mary,
Suffered under Pontius Pilate,
Was crucified, dead, and buried;*
The third day he rose again from the dead;
He ascended into heaven,
And sitteth at the right hand of God the Father Almighty;
From thence He shall come to judge the quick and the dead.

I believe in the Holy Spirit, the holy **catholic Church,
the communion of saints, the forgiveness of sins,
the resurrection of the body, and the life everlasting. Amen.

*The oldest manuscripts include "He descended into hell" at this point.

** "Church universal" may be used as an alternate phrase here.

The Nicene Creed

We believe in one God,
    the Father, the Almighty,
    Maker of heaven and earth,
    of all that is, seen and unseen.

We believe in one Lord, Jesus Christ,
    the only Son of God,
    eternally begotten of the Father,
    God from God, Light from Light,
    true God from true God,
    begotten, not made,
    of one Being with the Father.
    Through him all things were made.
    For us and for our salvation
    he came down from heaven,
    Was incarnate of the Holy Spirit and the Virgin Mary
    and became truly human.

For our sake he was crucified under Pontius Pilate;
he suffered death and was buried.
On the third day he rose again
in accordance with the Scriptures;
he ascended into heaven
and is seated at the right hand of the Father.
He will come again in glory to judge the living and the dead,
and his kingdom will have no end.

We believe in the Holy Spirit, the Lord, the giver of life,
who proceeds from the Father and the Son,
who with the Father and the Son is worshiped and glorified,
who has spoken through the prophets.
We believe in the one holy *catholic and apostolic church.
We acknowledge one baptism for the forgiveness of sins.
We look for the resurrection of the dead,
And the life of the world to come. Amen.

* "Church universal" may be used as an alternate phrase here.

This translation was recently done by the ecumenical English Liturgical Commission (ELLC).

A Statement of Faith

We are not alone, we live in God's world.
We believe in God:
Who has created and is creating,
Who has come in Jesus, the Word made flesh,
To reconcile and make new,
Who works in us and others by the Spirit.
We trust in God.
We are called to be the church:
To celebrate God's presence,
To love and serve others,
To seek justice and resist evil,
To proclaim Jesus, crucified and risen,
Our judge and our hope.
In life, in death, in life beyond death, God is with us.
We are not alone. Thanks be to God. Amen.

(UMH, 883)

Thanks and praise to You, Father, almighty Creator, merciful Lord, God of promise and fulfillment. From ancient times Your faithful people waited for the day of Your visitation, manifest at last when the time had fully come and You sent forth Jesus Christ, Your Son. Having seen His glory, we now wait for the day of consummation, when He will come again as Judge and King. Accept our praises this day in the name of the Father, who loves us to life; and the Son, who loved us to His death; and the Holy Spirit, who will love us to life eternal. Amen. (CC)

Almighty God, our heavenly Father, send the power of Your Holy Spirit upon us, that we may experience anew the suffering, death, and resurrection of Your Son, Jesus Christ. May your Spirit help us to know, in the breaking of the bread and drinking of the cup, the presence of Christ who gave His body and blood for us. Make us one in Christ, one with each other, and one in service to the world. Amen.

We do not presume to come to this thy table, O merciful Lord, trusting in our own righteousness, but in thy manifold and great mercies. We are not worthy so much as to gather up the crumbs under thy table. But thou art the same Lord, whose property is always to have mercy: Grant us therefore, gracious Lord, so to eat the flesh of thy dear Son Jesus Christ, and to drink his blood, that our lives may be made clean by his body, and our souls washed through his most precious blood, and that we may evermore dwell in him, and he in us. Amen. (BCP, 82)

The Body of our Lord Jesus Christ, which was given for thee, preserve thy body and soul unto everlasting life. Take and eat this in remembrance that Christ died for thee, and feed on him in thy heart by faith, with thanksgiving.

The Blood of our Lord Jesus Christ, which was shed for thee, preserve thy body and soul unto everlasting life. Drink this in remembrance that Christ's blood was shed for thee, and be thankful.

Scriptural Affirmations of God's Mercy and Grace

Hear the good news! "This statement is completely reliable and should be universally accepted: Christ Jesus entered the world to rescue sinners. . . . He personally bore our sins in his body on the cross, so that we might be dead to sin and be alive to all that is good" *(1 Timothy 1:15; 1 Peter 2:24, PHILLIPS)*.

"Who is in a position to condemn? Only Christ Jesus, and Christ died for us, Christ also rose for us, Christ reigns in power for us, Christ prays for us! . . . If a man is in Christ he becomes a new person altogether—the past is finished and gone, everything has become fresh and new" *(Romans 8:34; 2 Corinthians 5:17, PHILLIPS)*.

LEADER: Friends, believe the good news of the gospel.

PEOPLE: In Jesus Christ, we are forgiven.

"The Lord is merciful and gracious, slow to anger and abounding in steadfast love. . . . He does not deal with us according to our sins, nor requite us according to our iniquities. For as the heavens are high above the earth, so great is his steadfast love toward those who fear him; as far as the east is from the west, so far does he remove our transgressions from us" *(Psalm 103:8, 10-12, RSV)*.

"With everlasting love I will have compassion on you, says the LORD, your Redeemer. . . . I am He who blots out your transgressions for my own sake, and I will not remember your sins. . . . Return to me, for I have redeemed you" *(Isaiah 54:8; 43:25; 44:22, NRSV)*. Believe this gospel and go forth to live in peace. Amen.

14

"If God is for us, who is against us? He who did not spare his own Son but gave him up for us all, will he not also give us all things with him? Who shall bring any charge against God's elect? It is God who justifies, who is to condemn?" *(Romans 8:31-34a, RSV).*

"If we say we have no sin, we deceive ourselves, and the truth is not in us. If we confess our sins, he is faithful and just, and will forgive our sins and cleanse us from all unrighteousness" *(1 John 1:8-9, RSV).*

"If anyone does sin, we have an advocate with the Father, Jesus Christ the righteous; and he is the atoning sacrifice for our sins, and not for ours only but also for the sins of the whole world" *(1 John 2:1-2, NRSV).*

Hear the gracious words of our Lord Jesus Christ to all who truly repent and turn to him. "Come to me, all who labor and are heavy laden, and I will give you rest. . . . Him who comes to me I will not cast out. . . . The grace of our Lord Jesus Christ be with you." (Matthew 11:28; John 6:37, RSV; Philippians 4:23, KJV). Amen.

Almighty God, who doth freely pardon all who repent and turn to him, now fulfill in every contrite heart the promise of redeeming grace; remitting all our sins, and cleansing us from an evil conscience, through the perfect sacrifice of Christ Jesus our Lord. Amen.

"Surely he took up our infirmities and carried our sorrows, yet we considered him stricken by God, smitten by him, and afflicted. But he was pierced for our transgressions, he was crushed for our iniquities; the punishment that brought us peace was upon him, and by his wounds we are healed" *(Isaiah 53:4-5, NIV).*

"To him who loves us and has freed us from our sins by his blood, and has made us to be a kingdom and priests to serve his God and Father—to him be glory and power for ever and ever! Amen" *(Revelation 1:5, NIV).*

Responsive Call to Worship

LEADER: Let us join our voices to praise the spotless Lamb, Jesus Christ, who has redeemed us from sin and death.

Congregation: We, whom he has redeemed, will sing praises and shout for joy this hour;

LEADER: Because in Christ the Lamb we have redemption through his blood, the forgiveness of our sins in accordance with the riches of his grace.

CONGREGATION: Christ has redeemed us from the curse of the law by becoming a curse for us.

LEADER: Let us praise him saying,

UNISON: "Worthy is the Lamb, who was slain, to receive power and wealth and wisdom and strength and honor and glory and praise! . . . To him who sits on the throne and to the Lamb" we give worship this hour and forever and ever. Amen. (Revelation 5: 12, 13, NIV). (BWH, 72)

Prayer of Adoration

We approach your throne this hour, O God of all grace, with gratitude for the person and work of Jesus Christ. We come to turn our eyes away from ourselves and on to him.

We thank you for planning in eternity past to provide a means of redemption through the sending of your Son. You have provided an ample remedy for the alienation of sin. You have provided one who gave his life blood as our substitute. You enabled him to bear the wrath which we deserved for our disobedience. He willingly endured pain and suffering out of love for us and obedience to you. You made it possible for the blood of Christ to cover over our sins and remove their stain. You have freed us from the weight of guilt and from eternal condemnation. How can we help but love and adore you for the rest of our lives. You have made the ultimate sacrifice to redeem us.

So we come this hour to sing your perfections; to acknowledge what Christ has already accomplished on our behalf. Thank you that his work in past history continues to be efficacious in this century.

We glory in the cross because without the cross we would be helplessly lost. We come today resting all our trust for forgiveness and eternal life in the person and work of Christ. Even in the future eternal kingdom we will sing the glories of being redeemed by the Lamb.

Accept our worship this hour as we present it through Christ our Redeemer. Amen. (BWH, 72-73)

The Memorial

We shall do as our Lord commands. We proclaim that our Lord was sent by the Father into the world, that he took upon himself our flesh and blood, and bore the wrath of God against our sin. We confess that he was condemned to die that we might be pardoned and suffered death that we might live. We proclaim that he is risen to make us right with God, and that he shall come again in the glory of his new creation. This we do now and until he comes again.

(CRPH)

Preparation of the Elements

(As the minister breaks the bread and pours the cup)

MINISTER: The bread that we break is a sharing in the body of Christ.

PEOPLE: **We who are many are one body, for we all share the same loaf.**

MINISTER: The cup for which we give thanks is a sharing in the blood of Christ.

PEOPLE: **The cup that we drink is our participation in the blood of Christ.** (CRPH)

Prayer for Illumination

Lord, open our hearts and minds by the power of your Holy Spirit, that as the Scriptures are read and the Word proclaimed, we may hear with joy what you say to us today. Amen.

Prayer of Approach

Almighty God, our heavenly Father, send the power of Your Holy Spirit upon us, that we may experience anew the suffering, death, and resurrection of Your Son, Jesus Christ. May Your Spirit help us to know, in the breaking of this bread and the drinking of this cup, the presence of Christ who gave His body and blood for all. And may Your Spirit make us one with Christ, one with each other, and one in service to all the world. Amen.   (PH)

Words of Distribution

The body of our Lord Jesus Christ, which was given for you, preserve your soul and body unto everlasting life. Take and eat this in remembrance that Christ died for you, and feed upon Him in your heart, by faith with thanksgiving.

The blood of our Lord Jesus Christ, which was shed for you, preserve your soul and body unto everlasting life. Drink this in remembrance that Christ's blood was shed for you, and be thankful.

Silent Prayer

Almighty Father, whose dear Son, on the night before he suffered, instituted the Sacrament of his Body and Blood: Mercifully grant that we may receive it thankfully in remembrance of Jesus Christ our Lord, who in these holy mysteries gives us a pledge of eternal life; and who now lives and reigns with you and the Holy Spirit, one God, for ever and ever. Amen.   (BCP)

A Responsive Communion Meditation

LEADER: Jesus declared, "I am the bread of life. He who comes to me will never go hungry.

CONGREGATION: "If anyone eats of this bread, he will live forever."

LEADER: It is not with perishable things such as silver or gold that you were redeemed,

CONGREGATION: But with the precious blood of Christ, a lamb without blemish or defect.

LEADER: The blood of goats and bulls and the ashes of a heifer sprinkled on those who are ceremonially unclean sanctify them so that they are outwardly clean.

CONGREGATION: **How much more, then, will the blood of Christ, who through the eternal Spirit offered himself unblemished to God, cleanse our consciences from acts that lead to death, so that we may serve the living God!**

(John 6:35a, 51b; 1 Peter 1:18a, 19; Hebrews 9:13-14, NIV).

(STTL, 746)

Section Three

Foundational Scriptures for Communion

"Behold, I stand at the door and knock; if anyone hears My voice and opens the door, I will come in to him and will dine with him, and he with Me" (*Revelation 3:20, NASB*).

"I am the living bread that came down out of heaven; if anyone eats of this bread, he will live forever; and the bread also which I will give for the life of the world is My flesh" (*John 6:51, NASB*).

"Is not the cup of thanksgiving for which we give thanks a participation in the blood of Christ? And is not the bread that we break a participation in the body of Christ? Because there is one loaf, we, who are many, are one body, for we all partake of the one loaf" (*1 Corinthians 10:16-17, NIV*).

"Beloved, let us love one another; for love is of God, and he who loves is born of God and knows God. . . . In this the love of God was made manifest among us, that God sent his only Son into the world, so that we might live through him" (*1 John 4:7, 9, RSV*).

Christ our Paschal Lamb is offered up for us, once for all, when he bore our sins on his body upon the cross; for he is the very Lamb of God that taketh away the sins of the world: Wherefore let us keep a joyful and holy feast with the Lord.

From 1 Corinthians 5:7-8; 1 Peter 2:24; John 1:29

"'What no eye has seen, nor ear heard, nor the heart of man conceived, what God has prepared for those who love him,' God has revealed to us through the Spirit. For the Spirit searches everything, even the depths of God" *(1 Corinthians 2:9-10, RSV).*

"Come to me, all who labor and are heavy laden, and I will give you rest" *(Matthew 11:28, RSV).*

"God so loved the world that he gave his only Son, that whoever believes in him should not perish but have eternal life" *(John 3:16, RSV).*

"The saying is sure and worthy of full acceptance, that Christ Jesus came into the world to save sinners" *(1 Timothy 1:15, RSV).*

"If we confess our sins, he is faithful and just, and will forgive our sins and cleanse us from all unrighteousness" *(1 John 1:9, RSV).*

"If any one does sin, we have an advocate with the Father, Jesus Christ the righteous; and he is the expiation for our sins, and not for ours only but also for the sins of the whole world" *(1 John 2:1-2, RSV).*

Scriptural Affirmations of God's Mercy and Grace

Hear the good news! "This statement is completely reliable and should be universally accepted: Christ Jesus entered the world to rescue sinners. . . . He personally bore our sins in his body on the cross, so that we might be dead to sin and be alive to all that is good" *(1 Timothy 1:15; 1 Peter 2:24, PHILLIPS).*

"Who is in a position to condemn? Only Christ Jesus, and Christ died for us, Christ also rose for us, Christ reigns in power for us, Christ prays for us! . . . If a man is in Christ he becomes a new person altogether—the past is finished and gone, everything has become fresh and new" *(Romans 8:34; 2 Corinthians 5:17, PHILLIPS).*

LEADER: Friends, believe the good news of the gospel.

PEOPLE: **In Jesus Christ, we are forgiven.**

"The Lord is merciful and gracious, slow to anger and abounding in steadfast love. He does not deal with us according to our sins, nor requite us according to our iniquities. For as the heavens are high above the earth, so great is his steadfast love toward those who fear him; as far as the east is from the west, so far does he remove our transgressions from us" *(Psalm 103:8, 10-12, RSV)*.

"With everlasting love I will have compassion on you, says the LORD, your Redeemer. . . . I am He who blots out your transgressions for my own sake, and I will not remember your sins. . . . Return to me, for I have redeemed you" *(Isaiah 54:8; 43:25; 44:22, NRSV)*. Believe this gospel and go forth to live in peace. Amen.

"If God is for us, who is against us? He who did not spare his own Son but gave him up for us all, will he not also give us all things with him? Who shall bring any charge against God's elect? It is God who justifies; who is to condemn?" *(Romans 8:31-34a, RSV)*.

"If we say that we have no sin, we deceive ourselves, and the truth is not in us. If we confess our sins, he who is faithful and just will forgive us our sins and cleanse us from all unrighteousness" *(1 John 1:8-9, NRSV)*.

"If anyone does sin, we have an advocate with the Father, Jesus Christ the righteous; and he is the atoning sacrifice for our sins, and not for ours only but also for the sins of the whole world" *(1 John 2:1-2, NRSV)*.

Hear the gracious words of our Lord Jesus Christ to all who truly repent and turn to him. "Come to Me, all you who labor and are heavy laden, and I will give you rest. Him who comes to me I will never cast out. . . . The grace of our Lord Jesus Christ be with you." (Matthew 11:28; John 6:37, RSV; Philippians 4:23, KJV). Amen.

Almighty God, who doth freely pardon all who repent and turn to him, now fulfill in every contrite heart the promise of redeeming grace; remitting all our sins, and cleansing us from an evil conscience, through the perfect sacrifice of Christ Jesus our Lord. Amen.

"Surely he took up our infirmities and carried our sorrows, yet we considered him stricken by God, smitten by him, and afflicted. But he was pierced for our transgressions, he was crushed for our iniquities; the punishment that brought us peace was upon him, and by his wounds we are healed" *(Isaiah 53:4-5, NIV)*.

"To him who loves us and has freed us from our sins by his blood, and has made us to be a kingdom and priests to serve his God and Father—to him be glory and power for ever and ever! Amen." *(Revelation 1:5, NIV)*

Appropriate Hymns
for Communion

Alas! And Did My Savior Bleed	*Watts/Wilson*
All Hail the Power of Jesus' Name	*Perronet/Holden*
Alleluia, Alleluia Give Thanks	*Fishel*
Alleluia Sing to Jesus	*Dix/Prichard*
And Can It Be?	*Wesley/Campbell*
Ask Ye What Great Thing I Know	*Schwedler/Malan*
At Calvary	*Newell/Towner*
At the Cross	*Watts/Hudson*
At the Name of Jesus	*Noel/Williams*
Be Known to Us in Breaking Bread	*Montgomery/Gardiner*
Bread of the World	*Heber/Hodges*
Come, Sinners, to the Gospel Feast	*Wesley/Hursley*
Cross of Jesus, Cross of Sorrow	*Sparrow-Simpson/Stainer*
Crown Him with Many Crowns	*Bridges/Elvey*
Depth of Mercy	*Wesley/Gibbons*
Grace Greater Than Our Sin	*Johnston/Towner*

Hallelujah! What a Savior	*Bliss*
Here at Thy Table, Lord	*Hoyt/Sherwin*
Here Is Love Vast as the Ocean	*Rees/Lowry*
Here, O My Lord, I See Thee	*Bonar/Dearle*
I Come With Joy	*Wren/Webb*
I Know a Fount	*Cooke*
I Will Praise Him	*Harris*
I Will Remember Thee	*Montgomery*
Jesus Paid It All	*Hall/Grape*
Just As I Am	*Elliott/Bradbury*
Lead Me to Calvary	*Hussey/Kirkpatrick*
Let All Mortal Flesh Keep Silence	*Moultrie/Picardy*
Let Us Break Bread Together	*Traditional American Spiritual*
Lift High the Cross	*Kitchin, Newbolt/Nicholson*
My Savior's Love	*Gabriel*
Nothing But the Blood	*Lowry*
O Love Divine, What Hast Thou Done?	*Wesley/Woodbury*
Our Great Savior	*Chapman/Prichard*
The Head That Once Was Crowned With Thorns	*Kelly/Clark*
The Old Rugged Cross	*Bennard*
There Is a Fountain	*Cowper*

Under the Atoning Blood   *Lillenas*

What Wondrous Love Is This?   *American Folk Hymn*

When I Survey the Wondrous Cross   *Watts/Mason*

Appropriate Worship Songs for Communion

Above All	*Lenny Leblanc/Paul Baloche*
All Hail King Jesus	*Dave Moody*
Amazing Love	*Graham Kendrick*
By the Blood	*Chris and Diane Machen*
Come Into the Holy of Holies	*John Sellers*
Crown Him King of Kings	*Sharon Damazio*
Glory to the Lamb	*Larry Dempsey*
He Is Lord	*Anonymous*
Holy, Holy, Holy (Hosanna)	*Peter Scholtes*
I Remember You	*Christine Hayes*
I'm Forever Grateful	*Mark Altrogge*
Lamb of God	*Twila Paris*
Lord, I Lift Your Name on High	*Rick Founds*
Majesty	*Jack Hayford*
O for a Thousand Tongues to Sing	*David Binion*

O How He Loves You and Me	*Kurt Kaiser*
O the Blood of Jesus	*Unknown*
See How Mercy	*Gary Schmidt*
The Love of Christ	*Marty Parks*
There Is a Redeemer	*Melody Green*
We Shall Overcome	*Jack Hayford*
Wonderful Merciful Savior	*Dawn Rodgers and Eric Wyse*
You Are My All in All	*Dennis Jernigan*
You Are My King	*Billy James Foote*

Section Six

Appropriate Choral Anthems for Communion

Behold the Lamb   (arr. Kirkland)
   Lillenas Publishing Company   AN-1860

Behold the Man   (arr. Fettke)
   Lillenas Publishing Company   AN-2501

Come Celebrate Jesus   (arr. Parks)
   Allegis Publications   AG-1070

Come Expecting Jesus   (arr. Greer)
   Allegis Publications   AG-1024

Embrace the Cross   (arr. Linn)
   Lillenas Publishing Company   AN-2619

Grace   (arr. Parks)
   Lillenas Publishing Company   AN-1851

How Beautiful   (arr. Fettke)
   Lillenas Publishing Company   AN-8107

I Remember You   (arr. Parks)
   Lillenas Publishing Company   AN-2673

In Remembrance of Me   (arr. Wolaver)
   Allegis Publications   AG-1052

Isaiah 53/God Hath Provided a Lamb   (arr. Fettke)
   Lillenas Publishing Company   AN-2576

It's Still the Cross (arr. Kirkland)
Lillenas Publishing Company   AN-1846

Lift Up the Cross (arr. Allen)
Lillenas Publishing Company   AN-2638

Lord, From Your Hand (arr. Greer)
Lillenas Publishing Company   AN-2656

O Calvary's Lamb (arr. Parks, Fettke)
Lillenas Publishing Company   AN-2631

Remember the Lord (arr. Fettke)
Allegis Publications   AG-1039

See Them Come (arr. Parks)
Lillenas Publishing Company   AN-2660

Table of Grace (arr. Parks)
Allegis Publications   AG-1087

The Iniquity of Us All (arr. Parks)
Lillenas Publishing Company   AN-2640

There Is a River (arr. Parks)
Lillenas Publishing Company   AN-1872

Until He Comes Again (arr. Fettke)
Lillenas Publishing Company   AN-2669

Creative Ideas for Communion

As previously noted, traditions and customs in the serving and celebrating of Communion vary greatly from congregation to congregation. Thoughtful consideration of the service itself is always needed yet can present two very real dangers: tradition that lacks any vital relevance and innovation that eliminates mystery. Here are several ideas for the Communion service that help retain its deep meaning but are not so ritualistic that the individual worshiper loses the profound nature of the observance.

1. Consider the days on which you celebrate Holy Communion. In addition to when it is regularly scheduled in your church, are there other significant days to remember? Some of these might include Maundy Thursday, Worldwide Communion Sunday, the first Sunday of Advent, the first Sunday of Lent, Christmas Eve, and New Year's Eve.

2. Think of how the altar table is adorned—how the elements are presented. Is the table usually "set" with fine linen and brass or silver pitchers, plates, and candlesticks? For a visual change, use a "rougher" approach. Ceramic or earthenware vessels on top of a tapestry or burlap cloth make a definite impact and are, in reality, probably more like what Jesus used in initiating this sacrament. Also, consider using a bowl, pitcher, and towel. Another appropriate visual effect could be achieved by using live vines, fresh grapes, and stalks of wheat.

3. "Set" the table during the service itself. As appropriate music is played or sung, have clergy or laity (carefully rehearsed!) bring each of the elements to the unadorned table. The visual impact of preparing for the Lord's Supper is powerful.

4. Display or process with worship banners that portray symbolic graphics or appropriate phrases.

5. Consider different modes of distributing the elements. Is the congregation normally served in the pews? Maybe they could come to the front of the sanctuary to receive the bread and cup. Is your church accustomed to kneeling at the altar rail? Perhaps standing and receiving by "intinction" would be meaningful. *(Intinction is the ancient method whereby a piece of the bread or a wafer is received and then dipped into a common cup before eating. Thus, both elements are consumed at the same time.)*

6. Those who serve the elements can quietly speak words of assurance to those receiving. Phrases like "The body of Christ, broken for you" and "The blood of Christ, poured out for you" can follow the distribution of the bread and cup. If possible, speak the name of the person being served before the phrases are spoken. This reminds everyone of the incredibly personal nature of Communion.

7. In addition to distributing the bread and the cup, consider including some other tangible reminder of the love of Christ. Hand out printed cards that look like invitations and that include scripture passages such as Matthew 11:28, Isaiah 55:1, or Isaiah 55: 6. As the words, "The body of Christ . . ." and "The blood of Christ . . ." are spoken, follow this with "The invitation of Christ to you" and place the card in the hands of the receiver. Nails, as a reminder of our sins nailed to the cross of Christ, can also be distributed with great effect.

8. Sing music throughout the time the elements are served. The choir or worship team can lead in this and you may choose to alternate between instrumental, choral, solo, and congregational music. After all, Jesus and the disciples sang at the first Lord's Supper. Conclude with a victorious affirmation of the lordship of Christ.

Service Orders for Communion Worship

A Contemporary Celebration of Holy Communion

Prelude   Instrumentalists

Words of Invitation   Pastor or Worship Leader

The moment has come. A celebration is about to occur. The Master has prepared it. Only He could set this table; only He could send out the invitation, and He has done both. Come then, you who declare Jesus as your King. Come share in this celebration of the breaking of the bread and the drinking of the wine, and remember the sacrifice of Jesus that was the cost of setting of this table.

Songs of Celebration   Congregation

You Are My All in All—Jernigan
Lord, I Lift Your Name on High—Founds
Crown Him with Many Crowns—DIADEMATA

Greeting

The grace of the Lord Jesus Christ be with you.
And also with you.
The Risen Christ is with us!
Praise the Lord!

Passing of the Peace

Scripture Reading Pastor or Worship Leader

Isaiah 53:1-12
Philippians 2:5-11

Moments of Silent Meditation

The Lord's Prayer Congregation

Our Father, who art in heaven, hallowed be Thy name. Thy kingdom come, Thy will be done on earth as it is in heaven. Give us this day our daily bread, and forgive us our debts as we forgive our debtors. And lead us not into temptation, but deliver us from evil. For Thine is the kingdom and the power and the glory forever. Amen.

PASTOR: Hear the good news: Christ died for us while we were yet sinners; that proves God's love for us. In the name of Jesus Christ, you are forgiven!

CONGREGATION: **In the name of Jesus Christ, you are forgiven!**

Worship Songs Congregation

Freely, Freely—Owens
Wonderful, Merciful Savior—Rodgers, Wyse

Message Pastor

Serving of the Sacrament

(Customs and traditions concerning Holy Communion vary among churches. Adapt this portion of the service to your congregation's comfortable mode and procedure.)

Prayer After Receiving

You have given Yourself to us, Lord.
Now we give ourselves for others.
Your love has made us a new people;
As a people of love, we will serve You with joy.
Your glory has filled our hearts;
Help us glorify You in all things.

Song of Dismissal   Congregation

   Lord, Be Glorified—Kilpatrick

Postlude   Instrumentalists

A Service of Carols and Scriptures
for Holy Communion

Prelude   Organist

Introit   Choir

Call to Worship   Pastor and Congregation

   PASTOR: The grace of the Lord Jesus Christ be with you.

   CONGREGATION: And also with you!

   PASTOR: Christ has promised His presence in our midst.

   CONGREGATION: God is with us! Alleluia!

Carol, "Angels from the Realms of Glory"   REGENT SQUARE

Scripture Reading, Isaiah 11:1-9; 9:2, 6   Pastor

Moments of Silent Meditation

The Lord's Prayer   In Unison

   Our Father, who art in heaven, hallowed be Thy name. Thy
   kingdom come, Thy will be done on earth as it is in heav-
   en. Give us this day our daily bread, and forgive us our
   debts as we forgive our debtors. And lead us not into
   temptation, but deliver us from evil. For Thine is the kingdom, and the power and the glory forever. Amen.

   PASTOR: Hear the good news: Christ died for us while we were
       yet sinners; that proves God's love toward us. In the name
       of Jesus Christ, you are forgiven!

   CONGREGATION: In the name of Jesus Christ, you are forgiven!

Carol, "Hark! the Herald Angels Sing"   MENDELSSOHN

Scripture Reading, Isaiah 53:1-12   Pastor

Anthem or Special Music   Choir or Soloist

The Great Thanksgiving   Pastor and Congregation

> PASTOR: The Lord be with you.
>
> CONGREGATION: **And also with you.**
>
> PASTOR: Lift up your hearts.
>
> CONGREGATION: **We lift them up to the Lord.**
>
> PASTOR: Let us give thanks to the Lord our God.
>
> CONGREGATION: **It is right to give our thanks and praise.**
>
> PASTOR: It is right, and a good and joyful thing, always and everywhere to give thanks to You, Father Almighty, Creator of heaven and earth. And so, with your people on earth and all the company of heaven we praise Your name and join their unending hymn:
>
> EVERYONE: *Holy, holy, holy Lord, God of power and might;*
> *Heaven and earth are full of Your glory.*
> *Hosanna in the highest.*
> *Blessed is He who comes in the name of the Lord.*
> *Hosanna in the highest!*

Carol, "Angels We Have Heard on High"   GLORIA

Worship Song, "Emmanuel"   McGee

Distribution of the Elements

> *(Customs and traditions concerning Holy Communion or the Lord's Supper vary among churches. Adapt this portion of the service according to your congregation's comfortable mode and procedure.)*

Worship Song, "Wonderful, Merciful Savior"   Rodgers, Wyse

Prayer of Dismissal   In Unison

   Holy, merciful Father, in Your great love You have given us
   Jesus Christ, Your only Son and our only Savior. Send us
   from this place in the power of the Holy Spirit, that just as
   we have received the body and blood of Christ, we may be
   His visible presence in the world about us. Amen.

Benediction   Sung by All

   O holy Child of Bethlehem, Descend on us, we pray.
   Cast out our sin, and enter in; Be born in us today.
   We hear the Christmas angels The great, glad tidings tell.
   O come to us; abide with us, Our Lord, Emmanuel.

Postlude   Organist

Sources and References

The Book of Common Prayer. 1945. New York: The Church Pension Fund.   **BCP**

The Book of Worship. 1965. Nashville: The Methodist Publishing House.   **BW**

The Celebration Hymnal. 1997. Word Music/Integrity Music.   **CH**

Creative Communications. © copyright 1983. St. Louis.   **CC**

Engle, Paul E. *Baker's Worship Handbook.* © copyright 1998 Baker Books. Grand Rapids: Baker Books.   **BWH**

Job, Reuben P., and Norman Shawchuck. *A Guide to Prayer for Ministers and Other Servants.* Nashville: The Upper Room.   **GP**

Lutheran Book of Worship. 1978. Augsburg Publishing House.   **LBW**

From the *Psalter Hymnal,* © 1987, CRC Publications, Grand Rapids, MI 49560. 800-833-8300.   **CRPH**

Pastor's Handbook © 1991 Light and Life Communcations, Indianapolis   **PH**

Service Orders. Jackson, Miss.: Christ United Methodist Church.
                                                              CUMC

Sing to the Lord Hymnal. 1993. Kansas City: Lillenas Publishing Company.   **STTL**

Trinity Hymnal. 1990. Hosham, Pa.: Great Commission Publications.
                                                              TH

The United Methodist Book of Worship. 1992. Nashville: The United Methodist Publishing House.   **UMBW**

The United Methodist Hymnal. © copyright 1989. Nashville: The United Methodist Publishing House.   **UMH**